MIND OVER MATTER

A Handbook for Musicians to help you overcome Performance Anxiety

SUSAN WHYKES MA

Bloomington, IN   Milton Keynes, UK

authorHOUSE®

AuthorHouse™
1663 Liberty Drive, Suite 200
Bloomington, IN 47403
www.authorhouse.com
Phone: 1-800-839-8640

AuthorHouse™ *UK Ltd.*
500 Avebury Boulevard
Central Milton Keynes, MK9 2BE
www.authorhouse.co.uk
Phone: 08001974150

First published by AuthorHouse 1/24/2007

ISBN: 978-1-4259-6458-0 (sc)

Printed in the United States of America
Bloomington, Indiana

This book is printed on acid-free paper.

ACKNOWLEDGEMENTS

I WANT TO EXPRESS MY gratitude to my pupils who experimented with the material that now appears in this book, and for their honest feedback on the techniques that they tried out for me.

I thank my family for all their support, encouragement and enthusiasm.

I'd like to thank the Brain Gym people who inspired me to begin on this journey of life coaching.

Also I am grateful to Uncommon Knowledge and to Paul McKenna, who, just through his TV shows, opened up to me a world of hitherto unknown knowledge about the way the brain works.

CONTENTS

INTRODUCTION

"Anxiety is the gap between the now and the future"

Fritz Peris

ANXIETY CAN AFFECT MOST MUSICIANS at one time or another. Pre-performance butterflies in the tummy may be unpleasant but they can often give an important edge to a performance. Some players hover around the fringes of anxiety, but it is when we cannot make the switch from anxiety to excitement that the problems begin.

It's not your fault that you get very nervous before performing to others. It is the natural result of the way your brain programmes its information. By changing that programming in the unconscious mind you will be able to make the switch so that you are calm and in control next time you perform. You will learn how to relax and take things as if they are completely routine, and you will develop new ways of thinking and behaving that will guarantee your success.

There are no risks in doing the techniques in this book; just help and what sometimes appear to be quirky treatments. Who am I to be offering you all this? I am a music teacher by profession, and a flautist by obsession. If only I hadn't been so overtaken by nerves I might have been much more involved in live performance. As a teacher, my pupils often need help to overcome their anxieties as they go forward to exams and auditions. While doing my MA in Psychology for Musicians I researched performance anxiety, but all I concluded at that point in my life was that there were so many questions about the subject but no answers. At least, that is what I thought then, but now I know so much better. In finding the solutions in this book, I have tried them out on family, friends, pupils and myself. They have helped revise and refine these ideas, and I am grateful for their help.

Some tips and techniques have been included especially for the younger pupils to help them, and their parents, keep calm and relaxed before any big events, but this book is really aimed at those of us who have had our performances marred by nerves and anxiety attacks.

The remedies in this book are taken from several different therapies, and some, if not all, will help you. Some of the ideas in this book will not just help you cope with your fears, or just fill your mind with beautiful thoughts. In some cases they will not only get rid of the symptoms of anxiety but eliminate the underlying causes and maybe eliminate the signs of fear completely and immediately.

For your information, I have included useful books and websites at the end of this book in case you'd like more information, or see how these therapies work. This information I felt would be beyond the scope and need of this book. Many of the ideas in this book are readily available on websites across the world, but I have combined many in a fresh way to try to harness the healing powers of the body to overcome that debilitating performance anxiety.

To read and digest the knowledge in this book will take time. However, you have been practising your attitudes to performing since your childhood, so it will take more than just a few minutes to change your life around.

A word about the techniques:

Some of the techniques used in this book are quite complicated at first, so take your time to read them through and get comfortable with them before doing them for real.

Also, for the best benefits when doing the techniques, sit or lie comfortably with your legs and arms uncrossed.

A final thought before you start:

This book is about performing and stage-fright, and whilst this book and CD will help you overcome your fear of doing something in front of an audience, there may be issues in your background that have given rise to these fears that are associated with some other traumatic incident in your background, they are no substitute for professional guidance. In which case you should consult your doctor for recommended therapists.

PART 1

Getting to Understand Performance Anxiety –

The Science Bit

CHAPTER 1
Confidence

IMAGINE BEING VERY CONFIDENT, RELAXED and really alert next time you stand up on the stage or enter the exam room. Is this too outrageous to think about? Well this book will help you to achieve that.

Stop for a moment and really imagine how it would be if you were already in control of your performance nerves and you are doing your concert, completely at ease and in fact feeling as if this performance was merely routine.

How would you be feeling?

What kinds of things would you be saying to yourself?

How would you be standing or sitting?

Wouldn't it be wonderful to actually be that confident, relaxed musician you dream of being? If you practice these techniques you will become what you practice. Believe it or not, many of the skills you will need to develop the new confident you, you already have.

Positive Images

Giving the brain strong positive images of success will program it to think in these terms and makes success more likely. Unfortunately we learn much more quickly from our mistakes than from our successes, but we can unlearn the attitudes and behaviours we so quickly acquire. So many of us have practiced the opposite of confidence. We have worried that we are not quite the performer we hope to be and in this way we set ourselves up for a fall. We have felt unresourceful and scared when it is time to commit ourselves to the exam or audition and we automatically feel bad. Well, don't underestimate the power of the mind.

Walt Disney famously said, 'If you can dream it, you can do it'.

Imagining

Try this short but exciting bit of imagining:

1. Make yourself feel comfortable, either sitting or lying down, and imagine yourself as being quite confident.

2. Imagine a slightly more confident you in front of you now. Pretend you can float into this new, confident you, and feel how it is to be more confident, hear your voice, see how you stand, and really enjoy this sensation.

3. Now imagine that in front of you there is a bigger, more colourful and confident you. Float into this new you and enjoy all the sensations you can see, feel and hear. Notice your posture and the expression on your face.

4. Now imagine that in front of you there is an even bigger, even more colourful, even more confident you. Float into this new you and enjoy all the sensations you can hear, see and feel. Notice your posture and the expression on your face.

Come back out of the visualisation and see how you feel now. Do you feel a bit better about yourself? Do you feel that with more of these exercises you could possibly feel a little less nervous in future? Then please read on.

Worry

Experts have estimated that of all the things we worry about 40% will never happen, 30% are past, and all the worry in the world can't change them; 12% are needless worries about our health, 10% are petty, miscellaneous worries, leaving 8% for things that are legitimately deserve our concern and thoughts.

With the techniques in this book we can change the 40% anxieties so that we can feel confident and anxiety free, the 30% worries by altering the way we perceive them, and attack the 8% ones so that you can feel calm, relaxed, confident and looking forward to your next performance.

Keep practicing these techniques when you can and listen to the CD every day for about three weeks to really lock in the new attitudes and behaviours you will be learning in this book and you will find that not only can you dream it, you can be more confident and far more in control of any performance nerves.

CHAPTER 2
What Is Performance Anxiety?

Performance Anxiety

PERFORMANCE ANXIETY IS CONCERNED ABOUT the quality of our performance, a self-conscious, self-doubting awareness that hinders performance instead of helping.

Performance anxiety is a variety of anxiety that includes any or all of the following:

- fear,
- dread,
- stress,
- panic,
- nervousness,
- wariness,
- uneasiness,
- apprehension,
- worry about being tested.

Susan Whykes MA

Ripples in the pool

Performance Anxiety can be due to a tendency that is wired into us physically. It can be an accidental incident that begins a vicious circle of worry that interferes with performance and causes more reasons to worry. Imagine dropping a stone into a very large lake. The stone (performance situation) hitting the water causes ripples (a thought) which, if unchallenged because you are comfortable with the situation, allows the ripples to find their natural plane and the water becomes calm. However, if you are uncomfortable, then you begin to erect a barrier that bounces the ripples back on themselves, causing an internal chaos. It is vital to learn ways of breaking down these self-erected barriers so that you can go on to become a good performer. A musician is most likely to feel anxious when their attention is stuck on the consequences of going wrong or making a mistake, rather than focusing on the performance of the music.

Much research has been undertaken and there are thousands of articles, books, and websites about it. Theories abound about personality traits, human nature, and human development, but what help are they, when we are in the performance anxiety state? We know it isn't a life or death situation, but no amount of rationalizing with ourselves will dismiss our unconscious fears. What is it that we fear when we begin our piece, or enter the concert stage?

Recognising Performance Anxiety

Performance anxiety strikes in many ways, and while some of these will be all too familiar to you, some will be quite surprising. For instance, have you found yourself floundering as you try to select your audition piece, or putting off phoning your agent about work? Do you suffer from writer's block, or spend a lot of time drinking coffee rather than beginning work on your composition? These can all be classed as a type of performance anxiety. Not only are we often unaware of how anxiety prevents us from doing auditions or contacting agents, directors or producers but it can easily stop us from reaching our creative potential. The very act of creating can cause performance anxiety because creating can feel like a performance especially if the creation is going to be made public and thus evaluated and judged by others. It can prevent us from risking too much, thus staying in a safe comfort zone, when really we feel drawn in a different direction.

Have you ever found yourself over preparing for an event and yet still feeling under prepared when it starts? Is this because you in fact perceived the event as a performance without consciously realizing it? Or have you honestly performed to your potential whilst concentrating on how hard you are trying? Many kinds of performance go best if we can get into a 'zone' where conscious thought is a secondary element. Riding a bicycle is a good example of this, for when learning to ride there is a lot of conscious adjusting and balancing, but the best riding comes when the physical demands are well known and apparently forgotten.

Like Riding a Bike?

Consciously focusing on a task can actually interfere with performance. Going back to the example of riding a bicycle, if you focus on what you are doing you are very likely to end up with skinned knees or a broken arm. The cyclist who begins to worry about his riding is more likely to end up falling off the bike. This is the same for the musical performer. We need to be able to sideline our consciousness and let it become a part of the overall experience.

Alarm System

When the body perceives something stressful there is an immediate response by a hierarchy of glands that produce hormones such as adrenalin and noradrenalin. The purpose of these hormones is to put the body on alert to handle the emergency, known as the 'flight or fight' response. (More of this in the next chapter.) This happens within seconds without us having to think about any of it every time we meet something that gives us cause to fear, from meeting a lion or a bear to going on stage to perform.

The problems arise when our anti-bear, anti-lion alarm/alert system warns us of possible danger ahead that we might need to fight or flee from. This very system is counter-productive to performance and other endeavours, because rather than protecting us from whatever a bad performance might bring, the system actually makes those consequences more likely. If this wasn't enough, when we notice that our anxiety and nervousness about performance is interfering with our performance, the alarm/alert system warns us that the danger itself is causing problems and makes us even more anxious and gets even more in the way of our performance!

So the field that we are exploring is very large. It includes not only the stage fright that affects dancers, musicians and actors, but also creative block, and other presentation situations. It also affects amateurs, professionals, performers and non-performers. It can vary from mild feelings of discomfort, to complete paralysis.

To perform well

There are two aspects to performing well. The first is the performance of the activity itself, and the second is the impact that performance will have on others and yourself. If you want to perform really well, then it is this aspect that needs to disappear completely so that the only consideration left is that of doing the performance.

The root cause

You will be surprised to learn that maybe this all started when you were a child, when you were complimented for doing something well that you enjoyed doing. The next time you engaged in that activity you probably didn't feel so comfortable about doing it, and felt slightly less confident about it.

What happened? It was because the focus of your satisfaction in the activity shifted from internal, where you were experiencing the inner sense of enjoyment of being

11

'in flow' and at one with the activity, to an external one, as you experienced the response from outside. Once these signals became entangled, the more subtle inner satisfaction feelings can get pushed into the background. What we are left with is the sense of being judged, from whence performance anxiety is but a short step away.

In flow

Do you remember your driving test? So many people report feeling quite nervous about it and that whilst driving along they made a mistake quite early in the test. At that point they thought, 'Well that's it, I've failed now,' and they have just shrugged their shoulders and got on with enjoying driving around, only to hear the examiner say at the end of the test that they'd passed! That was because they relaxed after they had made the mistake, and focused purely on what they were doing. They became less self-aware, and it felt more as if it were a routine driving lesson.

Whilst you may be of a more nervous personality as a musician than other people, this does not mean that past experiences of performance anxiety are hard-wired into your brain. It is software, and therefore changeable. You will be learning how to control your performance nerves and will feel more at ease about playing or dancing for others. You will be learning how to make these activities feel as if they are merely routine, and any mistakes made will take on little significance.

CHAPTER 3
The Emotional Nervous System

THERE IS MUCH WRITTEN ABOUT anxiety and panic attacks. This is because they are part of being human. The sense of fear and panic have kept human beings safe for millions of years, allowed us to survive, evolve and succeed as a species. Long ago, our ancestors scanned the environment for danger, but somehow we assume ancient men were confident, brash, loud 'hunter/gatherers'. However, the way to survive in the hostile environment with animals larger, stronger, faster and more vicious was to avoid them as much as possible. Humans learnt to be quiet, timid and very careful. When it was necessary to tackle your aggressor or to run for your life, a wonderful mechanism activated. This is called the 'fight or flight' response. This involves emotions of fear, alarm and panic. The body is put on alert. The heart beats faster so that more blood can be rushed to the muscles and brain. Adrenalin also rushes to the lungs to allow for a maximum intake of oxygen. Blood is directed from your extremities to your vital organs, leaving your hands and feet cooler, and the skin going paler. There is less blood in your arms and legs, giving rise to lack of co-ordination, wobbly knees and undisciplined fingers. Your pupils dilate and more sugar is released into the system for more energy.

Emotions of fear, alarm and panic involve the entire nervous system but there are two parts of the nervous system that are significant for our purposes: the limbic system and the autonomic nervous system.

The Limbic System

This is a primitive part of the brain that evolved to keep you alive. It is concerned with 'all or nothing' thinking and making simple but fast decisions. When faced by a charging lion or an angry bear, you need to decide rapidly, 'Shall I stand and fight or run away?'

The limbic system is a complex set of structures that lies on both sides and underneath the thalamus, just under the cerebrum. It includes the hypothalamus, the hippocampus, the amygdala and several other nearby areas in the brain. It appears to be primarily responsible for our emotional life, and also has a lot to do with the formation of memories. In the drawing below, you can see the brain as if it were cut in half, and shows the part of the limbic system which is along the left side of the thalamus (hippocampus and amygdala) and just under the front of the thalamus (hypothalamus).

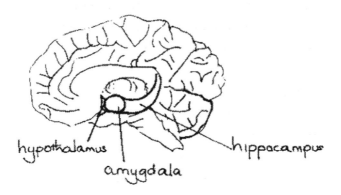

Cross-section of the brain

Hypothalamus

The hypothalamus is a small part of the brain located just below the thalamus on both sides of the third ventricle. The ventricles are areas within the cerebrum that are filled with fluid and connect to the fluid in the spine. It sits just inside the two pathways of the nerves from the eyes.

It is one of the busiest parts of the brain and is mainly concerned with keeping, or returning, the body at a 'set point', just like a thermostat functions by regulating the heat in your central heating system, heating up the room when it is cold and switching off the heat when the correct temperature has been reached. It is responsible for regulating your hunger, thirst, and response to pain, levels of pleasure, anger, aggressive behaviour and more. It also regulates the functioning of the other main nervous systems, parasympathetic and sympathetic, which means it also regulates things like pulse, blood pressure, breathing, sweating and other responses to emotional situations.

The other area of this system that is important to us is the amygdala.

Amygdala

The amygdala is actually two almond-shaped masses of neurons either side of the thalamus at the lower end of the hippocampus. They are involved in producing and responding to non-verbal signals of anger and fear that produce the 'freeze' reaction, such as sweaty palms and a tense mouth. Many gestures reflect the amygdala's function as we may flex our arms, lean away or angle away from people who upset us. Lips, shoulders and neck may tense as the amygdalas stimulate the brainstem circuits designed not only to produce protective facial expressions but protective postures like hunching over or curling up. It also prompts the release of adrenalin and other hormones into the bloodstream, thus stepping-up the avoidance response and disrupts the control of rational thought.

Fear is our friend! It has helped us respond to life-threatening situations and to predict dangers in the environment. However, nowadays, most threats are no longer physical but abstract. Once, you needed to be able to flee from a bear or a lion and needed energy quickly. When you are emotionally aroused, whether you are anxious, angry or excited, the brain changes the way it operates. The more emotion you have, the more you tend to operate through the limbic system, triggering ancient responses to physical threats. Today's threats are more abstract, such as waiting for your Grade exam day or waiting for house contracts to be exchanged. The limbic system is designed to make simple decisions fast. The more you try to solve a problem the more emotionally aroused you will become.

The Autonomic Nervous System

The second part of the nervous system to play an important and powerful part in our emotional life is the ***autonomic nervous*** system. It is actually composed of two parts which function in opposition to each other. The first is the sympathetic nervous system, which starts in the spinal chord and travels to a variety of areas of the body. Its function is to arouse the body for the kinds of response needed for 'fight or flight', in other words, running from danger or preparing for fighting.

Some of the effects you notice when this system is activated are:

- Dilation of the pupils
- Opening the eyelids
- Stimulation of the sweat glands
- Dilation of the blood vessels in large muscles
- Constriction of blood vessels in the rest of the body
- Increase in heart rate
- The bronchial tubes open up the lungs
- The secretions in the digestive system are inhibited

Anxiety produces effects many a nervous musician knows only too well:

- Little or no saliva produces
- All or nothing thinking such as, 'That's it, I've made a mistake, now I've failed!'
- Tense muscles
- Rapid breathing

The **parasympathetic** system operates in such a way as to counter all the above effects and bring the body back from the emergency status that the sympathetic system has put it into. This is the system we are going to be working on to calm the nerves, and get anxiety back into proportion.

(A third part of the autonomic nervous system is the enteric nervous system that controls the activity of the stomach. When you get sick to your stomach or feel butterflies when you get nervous, you can blame this nervous system.)

 If you can take away any one of the effects of anxiety, then the limbic system starts to switch off and the parasympathetic system calms the body down.

So to stop the panicky emotion you need to:

- Encourage saliva production....try chewing some gum
- Ignore the 'all or nothing' thoughts....try saying to yourself, 'It was only a slip, I'm doing all right'.

- Relax muscles….hence the restful CD and the other techniques in this book.
- Deliberately breathe in a relaxed way.

So to calm down, try this technique:

Breathing

When you are nervous you tend to gulp air, fine if you want to have lots of oxygen to enable you to run away from a lion or a bear, but not good for playing Mozart. When you breathe out, the parasympathetic system comes into play and that calms you down, so breathe out for longer than you breathe in.

Try breathing in while you count to five and breathe out while you count to seven. Use your tummy muscles to breathe with to make this really effective.

CHAPTER 4
Feeling the Power

AS I SAID AT THE very beginning, this book is not about positive attitudes and affirmations, although some of these will be used as anchors to your new confidence. The key to positive attitudes is not about thinking processes but about feeling. Whilst this may sound quirky, human beings are not just flesh and blood, but electro-magnetic energy too. Every nerve in our bodies is fired by minute amounts of electric energy, and this affects our whole being. Because of this electricity, we carry an electric charge around with us, and one could argue that if our charge is negative, we feel down, sad, low spirited and often bad or sad things happen to us. If we could change that charge into a positive one then we could feel like the world is our oyster, with limitless possibilities and full of fun, life and power. There is a way to affect these feelings, and here's how.

This is a four-step system which will require you to take a few minutes out from your busy life but which will revolutionize how you can make yourself feel.

Identify what you don't want.

There are so many don't want's in life; unfortunately we are surrounded by them:

- I don't want to drive in the snow
- I don't want to be in debt
- I don't want to look bad
- I don't want to make a fool of myself
- I don't want to play badly
- I don't want to feel nervous
- I don't want to mess up my performance again..........etc!

Sometimes they come disguised as 'if only's':

- If only I hadn't played so badly
- If only that man in the audience hadn't coughed
- If only I had spent more time practicing my entry
- If only I hadn't chosen that particular piece…

Sometimes they come in another guise altogether..

- I want to play well
- I want to lose my stage fright
- I want my hands to stop shaking.

Positive or negative?

This last list looks as if it should be positive, but really what you are saying is that, 'last time I didn't play well but this time I will'. Or, 'If only my hands didn't shake so much I would be in control on my flute playing and get a grip on myself'. Do you see how it works? One teacher was trying to avoid the winter 'flu so that she would be well enough to accompany her performers, so was saying things like, 'I need to keep well', and what happened? Yes, you've guessed, she went down with 'flu about two days before the event.

Identify what you do want

What we have to do now is try to find a way of expressing what we do want without any reference to the 'don't wants'. We have to change the feeling. If you have said to yourself in the past, 'I wish I didn't get so nervous when I am auditioning', try saying to yourself instead, (even if you have to pretend and fantasize about it), 'What would it be like if I had all the confidence in the world, how I would wow those judges, how I would play my exam pieces with style and musicality....'

What are your dreams, your hopes for yourself, even your smallest desires? It is all right to have them, and identify them. Do you feel a little excited, a little more confident, a little bit great about yourself, then:

Really let that feeling grow and grow

Let these feelings grow until you feel really good and excited and about to burst with pleasure.

So, feeeeel what it would be like to play your piano pieces without any nerves at all, and imagine how you will feel when you have finished and are taking your bow, with everyone in the audience clapping and cheering you. Imagine the flowers being pressed on you, and the people lining up just to shake your hand. Go on and enjoy that great feeling of pleasure. Don't let anything get in your way of feeling this moment. Don't allow any thoughts about how embarrassed you might be about the missed note on page 4 or how you fluffed up the double-tonguing…just feel that acclamation from others, and feel good about yourself.

Pretend

If you find this really hard to do then just allow yourself to pretend. Pretend that you are happy just for a moment, like when maybe you received your hard-earned degree. Allow yourself to pretend that that feeling of pleasure is growing, and imagine everyone around you congratulating you on how well you've done, and how thrilled they are for you. You will be grinning from ear to ear before you know it…

Smile

> Try this now.
> Just smile.
> Think about something that gives you pleasure, the first daffodils in your garden, little kittens tumbling over one another, the smile on your baby's face. Now smile. Just a gentle smile, not false or toothy grin type, a loving tender caring sort of smile that comes from within.

Can you sense a little feeling in your stomach or solar plexus, a gentle warm, fuzzy sort of feeling? This area of the body, about one inch below your navel and midway between your front and your spine is known in Japanese as '*hara*' and believed to be the central point of your body where your life-force is stored.

Think about that feeling and add to it a feeling of how you feel when you are appreciated for something, or if someone tells you they love you, or how good you are, (even pretend it if you need to) and let those feelings mix together and build.

Quite nice, isn't it?

 This 'hara' point is a very important part of the body. Quite often we find the thoughts about our fears and nerves in our heads, but try putting them into this point in your tummy, and feel the fears recede and the nerves calm.

When fear hits us, our bodies react by a sudden burst of electromagnetic energy causing the flight or fight reaction in the body, and we are hit with adrenaline. Well, when we make this feeling of a sudden burst of joy, or terrific feeling of pleasure we release into our bodies all kinds of positive, happy inducing chemicals which are really good for us, giving us energy and confidence, making us smile and feel good. So this 'feel' technique is worth working on for all kinds of situations, but we will be combining it with some other confidence boosting, and nerve-calming techniques that will change your performance life around.

CHAPTER 5
The Critic Within

THERE IS A LITTLE VOICE inside your head that chatters on, explaining and exploring, asking questions and answering itself, providing a running commentary on what you are doing, experiencing and feeling. It is automatic and unstoppable and often self-defeating.

Nobody would be allowed to speak to you the way you speak to yourself. If your performance falls short of perfect, you see yourself as a total failure. Your voice says, 'I've made a mistake, that's so typical of me!', or, 'I'm such an idiot', or 'I am so pathetic!'

Our Internal Voice

Our internal voice can be our friend but also our foe. It can give us encouragement and support one moment whilst making us uncertain and nervous the next. Our severest critic is ourself. Our internal voice gives us a harder time than any external person. Who else can get away with saying,

'I look dreadful today', or 'Stupid fool, you've gone and done it again!' Who else hammers away at us with cruel comments about how we messed up our exam pieces, or how we tripped over the steps onto the stage when everyone was looking?

As musicians we often find that we are happily playing our piece of music in a concert or an exam when the little voice in our head draws attention to some difficult bars coming up. Our focus is then diverted away from the piece and turns into a thought or a slight anxiety. We then lose the freedom of performance and concentrate instead on any tightening of our stomach or dryness of our mouth.

If this comes close to your experience then try placing focal points on the music....say about eight bars past the difficult passage.

Change the voice

Try this experiment:

Slow down that internal voice.

Now speed it up.

Try changing the tone of that voice to a silly voice.

Remember a time when someone made a comment to you that you didn't like.

Now speed up that voice and make it sound silly.

It doesn't seem so bad now, does it?

Do the same to your internal voice, and you will be smiling at how silly some of the things you say to yourself can sound.

The positive internal voice

Now you are going to make that internal voice work for you instead of against you. You can turn those negative comments into positive ones that reassure and comfort you.

Now close your eyes for a minute or two, and imagine there is a friendly mirror in front of you.

Look at yourself in it, and imagine someone that loves or deeply appreciates you standing next to you.

Hear all the lovely things they say about you, feel how much they love you. Give them time to tell you all about how wonderful they think you are, how wonderfully you play and how proud they are of you to be doing this performance.

Now come back out and go and look in a proper mirror, look at yourself eyeball to eyeball, and hear all that again inside your head.

Put these thoughts where your old internal voice was. Hear again all those lovely things you heard, feel all that love and respect. Let it flood over you and let those really good feelings soak into your very being.

Tell yourself, in your new confident internal voice, positive things like, 'I am very relaxed ... I am very confident...I enjoy playing my music ... I can dance with real flow...'

Try doing this daily, and your inner voice will cease being your critic and instead will become your best friend, helping you to become more confident about yourself very quickly.

PART 2

Getting Rid of the Past and Healing the Present

CHAPTER 6
Getting Rid of Past Memories

ONE OF THE BASIC PSYCHOLOGICAL rules in life is that you always get more of what you focus on. So, it seems reasonable that, if you keep on remembering past experiences of performance anxiety before an up-and-coming performance, you will naturally feel quite anxious.

1. Our past experiences of 'bad' performances stay in our memories. They can be bright, colourful and painful. Remember what happened in all its intensity; big, bright, close to you, and feel the pain.
2. Now make your memory go black and white, make it go smaller and smaller until it's about the size of a postage stamp, dark, black and white.
3. Make any voice associated with this memory speed up until it sounds fast and silly.

4. Make the memory get smaller and smaller and, with your internal eye, move it up and off to the left. Do this for each memory and you will soon be able to think about the past without the painful emotion.

Score your level

How severe is your anxiety level? If you had to rate it on a scale of 10 to 1 with 10 being the worst you have ever felt and 1 being almost unconcerned and no trace of upset, what would it be? Maybe you have a really bad memory of a concert you gave and how crushed you felt when, as far as you were concerned, it all went wrong. Your mind went blank, and you just couldn't remember what came next, or you played B flats in something that didn't need them...something you'd never done before. Or you just couldn't remember even what note your scale started on in your exam?

Perhaps you have a performance coming up soon, and you can already feel your heart racing at the thought of it...find the number on the scale of 1 to 10 that fits best with you. Really feel that anxiety. Don't be afraid of feeling the anguish; let your heart race, your mouth go dry.... just really focus on and feel that anxiety. You might like to jot the number down, because later you might be surprised at how bad you felt right now. Don't worry about how high a number you've written down, just be honest about how you feel about your anxiety right now. Even though the thought of this particular dread may be perturbing, don't worry; it will get better very soon.

Have you already experienced a bad attack of performance anxiety?

This technique is a tried and tested technique for getting rid of all types of past bad memories. It is quite time consuming, but it really is worthwhile if you have had a bad experience in the past that overshadows your present.

Try to imagine yourself sitting in a cinema or watching television with a still, frozen image on the screen.

Now, float out of yourself and imagine yourself watching this screen from behind yourself as if you were several rows back.

Next float back along your past until you find the incident of performance anxiety that you remember.

Run a film of yourself from before the event when everything was still all right, through the danger-zone and through to a point where you were safe again. (This may take a bit of time, but don't hurry, because this technique will undo that earlier damage.)

Now, play the movie backwards quite fast, from the time when you felt safe at the end of the performance back through time to before you even went on stage.

Run this movie again and again, faster and faster, forwards and backwards each time.

Come back out from your movie into the real world.

You will find that you have been able to experience that first event and coped with it.

Now try the first sequence again, and feel the difference.

CHAPTER 7
Your Own Personal Genius

NLP (NEURO LINGUISTIC PROGRAMMING) is the science and art of personal excellence; science because there are quantifiable methods and processes that allow for personal development and accelerated learning, and art because everyone brings their own unique style and personality to the process which makes it a unique experience for every person. The process that NLP employs is called modelling, and allows you to both understand and build on past successes so that you can discover your own personal genius. The topic of NLP is large, and we are only going to explore a small amount of it to collapse old ideas about yourself and build new strategies for conquering those performance nerves.

Visualisation

One very useful technique is to use visualisation. When you daydream about winning the lottery and how you would spend the money you will have thought in pictures or feelings rather than something that happens in words. This is called 'visualisation'. Visualising is a skill. It is the process of watching yourself on a screen in your mind's eye, consciously evoking and guiding daydreams in which you appear. Usually we will use visualisation towards a specific end because it can affect physical function.

Try a simple experiment:

Take a moment to think of a time when you felt really good about something.....at this stage it does not have to be related in any way to music.

Now think yourself back into that experience, noticing the sounds you can hear and what you can see. Notice in particular how you feel.

Now return to your present state and notice your breathing, your posture, and how good you feel.

Now repeat the process with a slightly uncomfortable experience. When you have remembered one, imagine yourself back there, and notice what you see, what you hear, and most important of all, how you feel.

Do not stay there very long, but come back to your present state and just notice the difference this memory has had on your breathing, your posture and your emotion.

Now, please try one of your feeeeeeling good inner smile activities from the previous chapter to sweep away the cobwebs of that last exercise and change your emotional state.

Influencing our bodies

The reason for doing that small experiment is to try and demonstrate how these past memories engage your whole body in changes of muscle tone, posture, and breathing and can contaminate your future experiences for minutes and sometimes even hours. As we go through life we are continually moving from one emotional state to another, and if we do nothing about this we are at their mercy. We can influence our emotional states and experience the freedom that can transform the quality of our lives. We cannot change what actually happened in the past, but we can change their meaning in the present and thus their effect on our behaviour.

Influencing our minds

Visualisation also accelerates the learning process. When you practice a skill you are running signals to and from your muscles and your brain, clearing and widening the neural pathways, clearly marking connections and intersections so that there will be minimal delays between translating the signals and co-ordinating movement.

Are you ready to get to work to transfer positive emotional resources from your past to be available in the situations that you are feeling negative about?

Well here we go.

Role Model

A really useful tip to help you with your performance anxiety is to imagine someone you really admire and respect. Alexander the Great modelled himself on the legendary warrior Achilles. Thomas a Kempis had perhaps a higher role model in mind, Stravinsky borrowed heavily from Mozart, and so the list can go on.

Try choosing a role model for yourself and then read the last paragraph in that person's voice, saying the words in your head.

Now imagine your role model doing what it is that you would like to emulate. Do this slowly and repeat it several times if you need to.

Now float into your role model's body and feel, see and feel what it is like for her/him to be doing that task or using that skill. Get the sense of what it is like for your model to be doing this task.

Repeat this technique until you feel what it is like to be your role model.

Make a Movie

Now you are going to use the power of your imagination to begin to build up a new image of yourself, in flow and at one with your performing activity.

Watch yourself in your imagination behaving the way you would ideally like to. If this is difficult, try watching your role model doing the behaviour instead.

Pretend you are Stephen Spielberg and watch a film of yourself playing superbly or dancing with freedom and flow just like you dream you could. Watch the scene as it unfolds before your inner eye, but don't get involved in the movie. You are the star as well as the director and you can edit the movie and the soundtrack until you are completely satisfied.

Then, when you are happy with the movie, step inside the image of yourself and run it through as if you are doing it, really enjoying every moment and allowing the feeling to confidence to grow and grow. Make everything vivid and bright, sharp and clear, loud and confident.

Anchoring for confidence

If we use the visualisation technique you have just tried but add a physical touch, called an anchor, we get a very powerful tool for helping our minds become free of performance nerves.

This is a bit complicated to do at first, so take your time to read through the instructions before you begin.

Firstly, find a comfortable place to sit or lie down.

Close your eyes and recall a time when you were completely confident. As you go back to that time, step back into that situation and remember it as vividly as you can, see what you saw, hear what you heard and really feel how you felt. Let this feeeeeling grow and grow. Try making the image brighter, larger, and sharper.

While you are vividly recalling this and when you feel that this memory is at its peak, slide a finger down the back of the corresponding finger of the other hand. This is called an 'anchor'. Take time to do this, and try to make it ten times better than you expected.

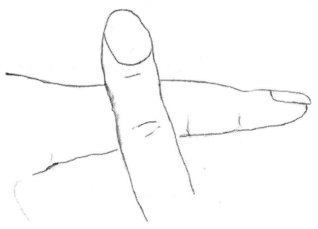

As the feeling fades, slowly release your anchor.

At this point you might like to add another positive emotion, for example, remembering a time when you played with enormous enjoyment, or feeling alert yet relaxed or really powerful.

Then repeat the steps above, still using the same fingers to anchor your positive feelings.

Now come out of these memories and just rub your hands together for a couple of minutes.

When you are ready, close your eyes again and think of the situation that you want these emotional resources in, just imaging that forthcoming audition, or that concert, and slide your finger over the back of your other finger just as you did when you were learning how to anchor.

On a scale of 1 to 10 with 1 being the best feelings and 10 being the worst, how does that last situation feel now? A good deal better, I'm sure.

The good thing about this technique is that you can trigger any helpful and positive state by repeating the steps above, sometimes recalling two or three more similar events that match your targeted one, to make a very positive state of mind, and then anchor this with any anchor that is not likely to be an everyday occurrence, (pressing the middle finger and thumb together, or squeezing an earlobe).

The next technique is a really powerful tool. It seems simple, but it is really effective at calming those performance nerves.

The wheel of fear

Think about the past performances when you were attacked by performance anxiety. Where did you feel the fear? Most people find it is in their stomach first and then it travels up to their throats and mouths. Give this feeling a colour.

Imagine there is a wheel in front of you and the wheel is going to spin the fear up from your tummy, up your chest and out of your throat and mouth.

As the wheel spins, the fear is spun out of your tummy. Imagine the colour streaming out of you, spinning faster and faster, and spinning out more and more fear, faster and faster.

Now choose a calm colour and this time let the calm spin into your tummy, slower and slower until the entire colour has left the wheel.

What level would you rate your fear at, with 10 being really anxious and 1 being really calm? You need to repeat the process until you feel the level is at about 3 or less.

Good fun this one, isn't it! Use it every time you feel anxious, whether it is because you are standing at the top of a slide, going into an interview, or going on stage.

Tap, Tap

In his book, 'Tapping the Healer Within', Roger Callahan explores healing of stress and emotions through tapping on certain acupuncture points. These are extremely powerful points on the body that can radically change the way you feel.

Now, what we are going to do next seems really bizarre, but it is amazing how effective this is. I want you to try out some places on your body you are going to tap. Then we will put them into a sequence that will change your anxiety level. Crazy! I know, but what have you got to lose by trying it out but your anxiety? Quite often the points you will be tapping will be sensitive. If they are, be gentle but firm, but don't worry if you can't feel any particular sensation when you are tapping.

Take your time to read this through first since there is quite a lot to take in.

You are going to use two fingers of one hand, (either one, it doesn't matter), and firmly but gently you are going to tap on these points, (keep focusing on that anxiety):

Tap at about 3 to 5 times per second:

1. Tap at the corner of the eyebrow just above the bridge of the nose. Tap here five times.
2. Under the eye...about one inch below the bone under your eye, (about where any bags under your eyes would be). Tap here five times.
3. Under the armpit. Ladies find this spot easy to find by tapping at about the centre of the bra under the arm. Men will find it is in line with the nipple. Tap here five times.

---

4. The collarbone. This is a bit tricky to find, so take your time to find it by tracing down the throat to find the collarbone notch and then moving straight down one more inch and across one inch. Tap here five times.

Tapping points.

5. Now tap the outside of your hand midway between the bottom of your little finger and your wrist with the fingers of the other. Tap here five times.

6. Now for a fun but complicated sequence:
   Tap the top of your hand.

Find the spot by making a fist with the hand, and running a finger between the knuckles of your ring and little fingers.

It will be down an inch from here.

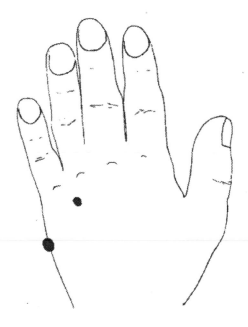

Keep tapping here while you:

- Open your eyes
- Close your eyes
- Open your eyes and look down to your left
- Now look down and to the left
- Circle your eyes quite quickly round in one direction
- Circle them back in the other direction

- Rest the eyes and hum quite loudly a few bars of a favourite tune with a nice big yawny round mouth.
- Count out loud from 1 to 5
- Hum again
  1. Now go back to the beginning of the sequence and tap at the beginning of the eyebrow.
  2. Tap under the eye five times
  3. Tap under the arm five times
  4. Tap the collarbone point five times

Now rate your anxiety level again. If it has gone down to 1 go straight to step 10, but if it has decreased significantly but not yet completely, repeat step 4 but then go from the top of the steps again. Keep focusing on and feeling your anxiety.

When you feel the anxiety level has dropped to 2 or below, finish the sequence with this final step:

- Tap the little finger spot again
- Holding your head still, move your eyes down.
- Tap the back of your hand (as in step 6) whilst you move your eyes upwards, not too fast.

Alternative Technique

There is an alternative method that you could use, should you feel the need to work on your anxiety levels again. This uses some other tapping points.

1. Think and feel your anxiety and note your anxiety level
2. Tap under the eye as before
3. Tap under the armpit
4. Tap at the beginning of the eyebrow at the bridge of the nose
5. Tap your collarbone point
6. Tap your little finger spot. You will find it on the inside tip of your little finger facing your ring finger just next to the nail

Now for a fun but complicated sequence:

7. Tap the top of your hand. Find the spot by making a fist with the hand, and running a finger between the knuckles of your ring and little fingers and down an inch. Keep tapping here while you:
   - Open your eyes
   - Close your eyes
   - Open your eyes and look down to your left
   - Now look down and to the left
   - Circle your eyes quite quickly round in one direction
   - Circle them back in the other direction
   - Rest the eyes and hum quite loudly a few bars of a favourite tune with a nice big yawny round mouth
   - Count out loud from 1 to 5
   - Hum again

8. Now go back to the beginning of the sequence and tap under the eye five times
9. Tap under the arm five times
10. Tap at the beginning of the eyebrow five times.
11. Tap the collarbone point five times
12. Tap the little finger spot again

Now rate your anxiety level again. If it has gone down to 1 go straight to step 13, but if it has decreased significantly but not yet completely, repeat step 4 but then go from the top of the sequence again. Keep focusing on and feeling your anxiety.

When you feel the anxiety level has dropped to 2 or below, finish the sequence with this final step:

13. Holding your head still, move your eyes down. Tap the back of your hand (as in step 7) whilst you move your eyes upwards, not too fast.

PART 3

Three Weeks to Go

CHAPTER 8
Our Past, Present and Future

1 Timetabling the Future – by viewing the past

IN ORDER TO PREPARE FOR your future performance, you need to break your preparation down into do-able chunks. For example, if the exam or event is in a year's time then you have weeks to prepare. These weeks can be broken down into smaller, workable chunks like snapshots. The benefit of this is that you will be setting in place building blocks to your performance that will ensure that you will be fully prepared.

The way we view time is important. Difficult or unhappy times in the past affect our quality of life in the present, but also our hopes and fears for the future can paralyse us in the present. We know, only too well how, weeks before the event we can feel nervous about our forthcoming performance. There is the present where all our personal history and possible futures converge.

So firstly you need to establish how you perceive your past, present and future in your mind's eye.

Try imagining your life on a line through time, stretching from the distant past to the distant future. How do you perceive this line?

Does it stretch straight behind you to straight in front, or is the past over, say, behind your left shoulder and the future stretching over your right shoulder, that is in a diagonal from south-west to north-east?

Think about a simple repetitive task that you do very often like brushing your teeth and think of a time five years ago when you did this, and now repeat this but only one week ago, and now today.

Now think about doing it one week in the future, and again, but in five years' time.

Now you can see how you perceive your timeline.

You will be using this timeline in the next technique to help you build a series of pictures that your unconscious mind will use like a road map. You will need to have small goals that act as landmarks for your unconscious mind to recognise as you work towards that future performance. These goals are like a series of snapshots, but you will build up the road map in reverse order, starting with the final performance picture, and working backwards through other steps that you need to achieve on your way to that final event.

Snapshots

1. Now imagine yourself one year in the future and you have had the best performance of your life with everything going just as you wanted. Ask yourself about what has happened in your career, what amazing pieces of music have you played, what new attitudes and behaviours you have taken on board?

2. Make a snapshot that shows in picture form all that you most want to happen in your positive future performance. Make sure that you are happy and positive in your picture.

3. Make the picture really big, bright and vivid.

4. Now do the same thing for a snapshot for a few weeks before that first picture. This one will be a little smaller than the first.

5. Now do the same thing for a few weeks before the last snapshot only making this one a bit smaller than before. So now you have several snapshots connecting your present to your future, getting larger and larger with bigger and better things happening as you go through them.

6. Now you need to take a little time to look at these pictures with your internal eye and let your unconscious mind dwell on your pictures.

7. Next, let yourself go into each picture and allow yourself to really feeeeel and experience it. What does it feel like to have everything you always wanted?

8. Let yourself come back to the present and enjoy feeling confident in your future. Let your unconscious mind dwell on the road map you have just created and look forward to tomorrow feeling positive and enthusiastic about it.

2. Mental rehearsal

Secondly, you will need to mentally rehearse the music and your performance through in your mind. Your imagination is such an unbelievably powerful tool that you can control to bring about huge benefits.

1. Visualise yourself doing that up-coming performance.
2. Concentrate on the music that you have to play or the dance steps you will be doing. Run through it in your imagination, in detail. Notice how easy it is becoming as you become more acquainted with the notes. This frees you up to get yourself engrossed in the interpretation. You are totally free to imagine yourself as you would love to play, with no limitations, and with complete confidence. You can be the musician you always wanted to be.
3. Enjoy the musical opportunity. Actively change your perception and emotions to make yourself feel very positive.

4. Identify that up-coming performance and make it feel that it will be a positive, beneficial experience. Let the image become bright and vivid, loud and clear, and make an anchor with a fingertip rubbing your ear.

5. Look up and right and construct an image of something you want to achieve in the future taking into that picture all the feelings, pictures and words that you experienced in step 4 that were helpful.

6. Once you have established this new picture in your mind, do your favourite anchor from chapter 7 to lock it into place.

The entire process lets you learn from the past and free your expectation of the future from the grip of past failure.

3. Think and feel positively

Thirdly, you need to think of yourself in a positive, affirming way.

Confidence has little to do with experience but a lot to do with your mind. So you need to prepare your mind for the forthcoming performance.

1. Imagine yourself as the truly confident performer you want to be. Imagine how you would speak, stand, how your nerves would be, how else you are feeling.

2. Imagine your positive, encouraging internal voice telling yourself how confident you are now.

3. Now tell yourself out loud how confident you are, and how good you feel.

4. Imagine a circle on the floor in front of you and fill this circle by standing in a confident posture, speaking to yourself with a confident internal voice. Add in playing or dancing music with passion and by thinking about a cause you feel deeply passionate about and let these feelings flow into your body.

5. Step into this circle and let these feelings flow through your whole body, visualizing yourself doing your performance the way you want.

6. If you feel the image starting to fade, step out of the circle and

7. Re-feel the emotions and then step back in.

8. Repeat steps 3 and 4 until you automatically feel the way you want to.

As the performance draws closer, remember to listen to the CD to help your mind relax and prepare.

CHAPTER 9
Daily Exercise

WE HAVE COVERED A LOT of techniques, but try to make time every day for these, because these are the most important:

5 Minutes a Day:

Minute 1:

Run your movie of success; make all the images really bright, vivid and clear.

Minute 2:

Look into your friendly mirror.....but first close your eyes and think about someone who loves you and admires you and imagine yourself being in their body seeing yourself through their eyes.

Minute 3:

Looking into the mirror, look into your eyes and tell yourself about all your positive attributes.

Minute 4:

Do your confidence anchor

Minute 5:

Take a minute to write down any inspired actions that came to you whilst doing the previous minutes.

Listen to the CD

CHAPTER 10
Performance Time

Before the performance:

1. Listen to the CD.
2. Remember your snapshots of your future to put in place your building blocks towards your performance.
3. Mentally rehearse your music and performance.
4. Go over your positive self-imagery and confidence booster techniques.
5. Make your internal voice say good things to yourself.
6. Change your fear into excitement by doing your 'wheel of fear'.

Now find a quiet place in your mind:

Closing your eyes, with every out breath count down from 10 to 1. When you reach 1 imagine in your mind's eye that you can see a door.

Open the door and walk through where you can create a unique place of relaxation. For example, if you like to be at a beach, then create the beach and find a nice spot to sit or lie.

Notice all the time the sun in the sky and how the warm air brushes past your cheeks, and warms your skin.

Notice how the sea sounds, as the waves break on the shore and the sound as the sea sucks back before the next wave. Feel the comforting sand in your hands and how it feels on your feet. Hear the birds in the sky and enjoy their songs and chirps.

Notice the clouds floating in the sky, how they just love to perform without fear or self-awareness. Become engrossed in the scene and examine your goals as you experience the beach.

Take your time here.

In this state of relaxation you can imagine your future performance, how you will play with beauty and serenity.

Visualise the event, the way you enter the exam room or stage; imagine the music as you play it in your mind; imagine how beautifully you interpreted the music.

Imagine the way the audience cheer and clap. Give yourself permission to make some mistakes, but flowing through the music despite them.

When you have enjoyed how your music has flowed and how in the 'zone' you were, count down from 10 to 1 to come back out.

PART 4

For Younger Performers
(and nosey adults too)

CHAPTER 11
Tips for practice and tips to calm the nerves for younger pupils

SOMETIMES WE GET STUCK TRYING to learn something. Here are a couple of tips to get over that problem:

1) Try and visualize what it is you are trying to learn. Imagine your fingers touching the piano keys or dancing those steps. If you can't, then you know you have a problem. You will need to go over the passage again in much smaller bits, watching your fingers, and then doing it without any sounds, (i.e. try playing your piece with your fingers on the piano lid or a table top) until you can visualize that little bit, and then go on to the next little bit and work on that.

2) Practice at a speed that will allow you to do your music perfectly, that is, really slowly. You will find that, once you can play the passage without hesitation and fluently, the speed will naturally build up. Now go back to tip 1 and try the visualization technique to lock in the passage into your mind.

If you are feeling bad, and want to get unstuck all you have to do is to look up for a few minutes, keeping your head still. Look at the clouds, sky or just the ceiling. Your goal is to keep focused on looking up for two minutes and you'll soon see the bad mood evaporate.

If you are feeling *really bad and low*, try keeping your head still and rolling your eyes in a wide circle clockwise for two minutes and the counter-clockwise for two minutes.

Try this easy idea to calm yourself if you are feeling nervous:

There are two slightly raised bumps about 2 –3 inches above the eyes on an adult, known as the frontal eminences.

---

1. Sit down and get comfortable.
2. Lightly place the pads of your fingers of one hand over these eminences, gently stretching the skin. You may feel a slight pulse here. You may notice that the pulse from one bump is not the same as the other bump, but that is quite normal, especially if you are nervous or worried.
3. In your mind, go over the situation that is worrying you. It might be something that has already happened, or something coming in the future. Relive it or pretend it in all the detail you can, making all the images you see in your mind as clear and vivid as you can. If you can, think of it as if you are making a video diary of the event.
4. Think hard about all the negative things that you can, but don't worry if you can't think of all the details; your brain will fill in the details for you.
5. Play the video again, and once more.
6. Find a statement that is positive and sums up what you really want (remember our want's and don't wants from chapter 4).

---

7. Say your statement, (e.g. 'I will play in a calm way', or you could find a trigger word that sums up your want or role model), and roll your eyes first in a very slow, wide circle in one direction and then back in the other.

8. You should, by now, be feeling that the event is less important, or a bit foggy, or even disappeared altogether. You may find that you yawn, or sigh or simply take a deep breath. This shows that you have succeeded in changing how you feel about the event. This might have taken 20 seconds, or ten minutes, it doesn't matter how long really.

 Parents can try placing their fingers over the frontal eminences of a child who has woken from a nightmare or is sick.

You can try to talk to both sides of your brain! Your left side is the logic brain and is in control of verbal and analytical skills. It receives input in a similar way to a computer. It will need positively worded suggestions. The right side is the gestalt brain. This is our artistic brain, and houses our appreciation of rhythms and shapes. It likes statements made in a negative way.

A good way into the positive statement is: 'I'll get along fine without any anxiety', and into the right brain, 'There is no longer any need to be nervous'. (This side needs a 'no' in the statement for some reason.)

Now take your middle fingers, holding back the little finger with your thumb. Tap with the finger pads with a firm, rapid rhythm of about two beats a second. Use your left fingers for your left ear and the right fingers for your right ear.

Start tapping just in front of the ear, one third of the way down from the top. Tap up and over the ear, down behind it to the end of the mastoid bone. The path you tap is like the shape of your ear but about half an inch out from it on a bony ridge you may be able to feel.

While you are tapping your right ear, you say the negative statement with the 'no' in it, and when tapping the other side say the positive statement.

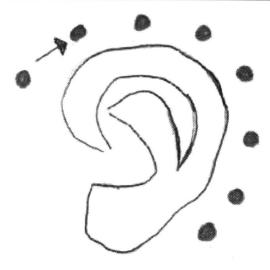

You might find that you do not need to do both sides, but you probably will sense which side you might need to do again on other occasions.

Amongst other really good ideas for exercising your brain the Brain Gym people have a great technique for getting yourself co-ordinated and your body ready to work.

Try to touch your left elbow on to your right knee by twisting your upper body round to the right as you do it, and then do it the other way, touching your right elbow on your left knee, again, twisting the body to the left to do it. Do this several times.

Then try touching your left hand to your right ankle behind your back, giving a good swing to the body as you do it, and then touch the right hand to your left ankle behind your back. Do this a few times too.

 Remember, that your body is mostly water, and to keep your brain active and alert, drink plenty of fresh, plain water

PART 5

Final Thoughts

CHAPTER 12
Final Thoughts

I AM SURE YOU WANT to know how quickly you will change. There is no easy answer because these techniques will build gradually. The more you practice the better you will become, but there is a pace of change that is right for you. Your unconscious mind has taken onboard so many new ideas, attitudes and behaviours that you need time to take all this on board. However, having said that, your friends and family may well notice changes in your confidence levels and behaviour before you do.

Keep practicing as many of these techniques as you feel have really resonated with you, and keep listening to the CD for at least three weeks prior to the performance, and top up before any future performances.

Enjoy your performing.

Enjoy your success.

With every best wish,

Susan Whykes

BIBLIOGRAPHY

AS PROMISED HERE ARE SOME useful books and web-sites that you may find useful:

Callahan,Roger.J: *Tapping the Healer Within*: McGraw-Hill, New York:2001,

Grabhorn, Lynn: *Excuse me, Your Life Is Waiting*: Hodder and Stoughton, 2000

Maisel, Eric: *Performance Anxiety*: Back Stage Books, New York, USA: 1997

O'Connor, Joseph, and Seymour, John: *Introducing NLP*: HarperCollins, London: 1990

Topping, Wayne: *Stress Release*: McNaughton and Gunn, Michigan, USA. 1985

www.Hypnosis Downloads.com

www.healingmusic.org

www.performance-anxiety.com

The relaxation track for this book is available as either a downloadable MP3 file or as a CD from www.audio.hypnotation.co.uk/audio

ABOUT THE AUTHOR

SUSAN WHYKES has an MA in Psychology for Musicians with Sheffield University. Part of the degree course was spent researching into aspects of Performance Anxiety. This raised many questions but found few solutions. Whilst working as a full-time music teacher and Tutor Mentor with Essex Music Services she has identified techniques used in sports pyschology and other sources of life enrichment and has used them to great benefit with her pupils and peers.

Lightning Source UK Ltd.
Milton Keynes UK
27 December 2009

147929UK00001B/67/A